Bootleggers, Bottles & Badges

The more sinister side of the so-called "Model Town of Clarkdale, Arizona"

D1608151

Peggy Hicks

Dedication

This book is dedicated to:

Those of you who might be curious about Clarkdale's history. Give yourself a ride through the pages of this book. Learn about the little-known history and folklore of the town of Clarkdale during its conception.

Copyright

Authors Note

The research materials for this book are a blend of facts and legends and centered on the "Prohibition Era aka Roaring-Twenties." The information has been drawn from many sources including newspaper articles, historical societies, libraries, archives and the old Clarkdale City dumps and my own experiences during my 35 years as a Clarkdale, Arizona resident.

Introduction

Clarkdale is a small town in Central Arizona on Historic Route 89A. Clarkdale was founded in 1912. It was built as a company smelter town for the employees of William A. Clark's Jerome copper mine. It was publicized for all intents and purposes as a "Model- Town" with model citizens. The town had everything a resident would want. But maybe, just maybe that was all hype. Records show Clarkdale also had a sinister side.

Chapters

Chapter 1: **Master -Planned Town**

Chapter 2: **Construction Begins**

Chapter 3: **Arizona Territory**

Chapter 4: **Oh Please Say It Isn't So**

Chapter 5: **Old Timer's Gold Nuggets**

Chapter 6: **Henry's Horse Feed Hooch**

Chapter 7: **The Volstead Act**

Chapter 8: **Close the Town Down**

Acknowledgments, Photos, Illustrations, References, Newspapers, Author's Books

Master-Planned Town

Chapter One

This book centers on the period between 1915 and 1930 during prohibition and highlights the more sinister side of the so-called "Model Town of Clarkdale".

We have all heard about the bootleggers, prostitutes, murders, and mayhem just four miles up the hill in Jerome Arizona. As a matter of fact, in 1903 a New York newspaper described Jerome as **"The Wickedest Town in the West."** Clarkdale on the other hand was supposed to be the "Model Town."

Was Clarkdale really a virtuous community? I took it upon myself to find out. I researched the old newspapers and archives. I also dug up a few clues in the form of discarded bottles that had been left behind in the Clarkdale dumps, proving that Clarkdale also had a sinister side.

Oh, please, say it isn't so. Clarkdale was supposed to be the "Model Town". And for the most part, that was true. However, some criminals went to great lengths to stay one step ahead of the law. Yavapai County Sheriffs busted moonshiners, jailed opium users, and solved murder cases in the small town of Clarkdale.

Senator William A. Clark

William A. Clark named his model town after himself, calling it Clarkdale. It was founded in 1912, the same year Arizona became the 48th state. Most towns in Arizona grew haphazardly in an uncontrolled fashion, but Clarkdale would be different. It is known as Arizona's first "master-planned" town.

Originally, Clarkdale was founded to provide housing and services for the employees of the United Verde Copper Company. The town had sewer, electricity, good water and even telephones. Clarkdale had wide streets with parkways, a central park and every convenience one could think of.

William Clark was a small wiry man with fiery red hair and a beard. With his boots on, he stood about five and a half feet tall and weighed a mere 135 lbs.

He was seldom seen without his swallow tailed coat. He was a senator, a banker, a merchant, a miner and was a millionaire by the time he was 30 years old.

William Clark had married his childhood friend, Katherine Stauffer in 1869. Together they had seven children. By 1878 Katherine and their children lived in Europe. Clark commuted across the Atlantic every winter to visit them and maintained a long distance relationship. Katherine died in 1893.

William Clark's original base of operations was in Butte, Montana. He lived in Montana for over forty years. By 1900, he was considered to be one of the richest men in the world. His fortune was estimated at about 50 million dollars. No doubt William A. Clark was a brilliant business man and entrepreneur, but his moral code was lacking.

He was shamelessly and constantly fixated on power and notoriety. With power and riches, however, often come corruption and feelings of entitlement. This was without a doubt, William Clark.

Clark's debatable romantic life gained attention during his Senate term in 1904. It was reported that he was quite fond of seducing young women.

For example, Hattie Rose Laube of Butte, Montana, who was helping Clark with his campaign, claimed that Clark had promised to marry her while the two traveled around Europe.

Another woman, Kathryn Williams also from Butte and 40 years his junior, claimed she exchanged sexual favors for his "financial sponsorship." Clark had paid for her acting school. Kathryn Williams later became a well-known actress in silent films.

Another Butte Montana woman named Mary Mc-Nellis sued Clark for $150,000 claiming that Clark had seduced and impregnated her and falsely promised her marriage.

Clark also started a relationship with a young woman named Anna La Chapelle. He sent her to France when she was 16 years old to study music.

In 1904, The U.S. Senator William A. Clark shocked other politicians when he announced his marriage to Anna La Chapelle, the daughter of a rough and tumble boarding house madam in Butte, Montana. No record of this marriage, however, has been found and most think it was just a face-saving hoax.

Anna La Chapelle and Baby

To the public, this salacious story of sexual attraction and the power of money on an astronomical scale were irresistible and the newspapers certainly took note.

Anna La Chapelle was only 23 and Clark was 62, almost 40 years her senior and old enough to be her grandfather. Anna had become pregnant with his child Andree in 1901, a miscarriage in 1903, and a third child Huguette born in 1906.

Left to right – Andree Clark, Senator Clark, Huguette Clark

More astonishing is Senator Clark's own children from his first marriage had no idea that they had a half-sister who was now two years old, until their father, William Clark announced it in 1904.

Over the years, Clark fathered at least nine children with two different women. His youngest child, a daughter, Huguette, was born in 1906.

Huguette outlived 5 of her lawyers and died at the age of 104 in 2011. She had tickets on the Titanic and was still living on 9/11 when the New York towers fell. She lived most of her life as an eccentric recluse. She left behind a fortune of more than $300 million.

William Andrew Clark wanted to become the senator of Montana. With all his resources at hand, he figured one way to get elected to the Senate was to "buy" as many votes as possible. And that's exactly what he did. It was reported that Clark bribed many voters with a thousand-dollar bill, spending more than four hundred and thirty-one thousand dollars to become the Senator of Montana.

Envelope with ten $1,000 bills with William A Clark's Initials

In a high-pressure, well-organized scheme, Senator Clark's agents had paid mortgages, purchased ranches, paid debts, financed banks, and blatantly presented envelopes of cash to legislators.

For some potential voters, they were simply handed an envelope full of cash. The larger bribes were usually paid in $ 1000 bills. When he was confronted concerning his bribery scheme, he said, **"I have never bought a man who wasn't for sale"**.

The corruption of his election contributed to the passage of the 17th amendment.

The U.S. Senate refused to seat Clark because of the 1899 bribery scheme, but a later senate campaign was successful and he served a single term from 1901 until 1907. Clark demanded he be called Senator William Clark from then on.

Mark Twain

In a 1907 essay, Mark Twain said, "Senator William Clark is as rotten a human being as can be found anywhere under the flag. He is a disgrace to the American nation, and anyone that helped send him to the Senate should have known that his proper place was in the penitentiary with a ball and chain on his leg. To my mind, he is the most disgusting creature that the republic has produced since Tweed's time".

Main Street,
Jerome, Arizona

Jerome, Arizona- 1895

William Clark purchased the United Verde mine
in Jerome in 1888. Extensive underground and
surface developments were undertaken to work
the ore which was of notable richness in copper,
silver, and gold.

These developments were along the upper
reaches of Bitter Creek Gulch north of the
present town of Jerome, Arizona. His mine
became known as the richest individually owned
copper mine in the world.

At one time Clark was netting over a million dollars a month in his Jerome operation. That's a lot of money even in today standards.

Clark did have his share of troubles. He could not put out the fires burning in the underground tunnels of Jerome. Not only were the timbers burning, but sulfured ore was highly combustible and the mine shafts were caving in.

These fires burned underground for more than 20 years. Geologist told him the best way to put out the fires was with an open pit operation directly over the underground fire.

The problem was his smelter was smack dab in the middle of where the open pit operation needed to be. In other words, his smelter needed to be moved.

Construction Begins

Chapter Two

Photo of Senator William A. Clark inspecting proposed site of Clarkdale Smelter in 1910.

Left to right -- Senator, W. A. Clark -- T. C. Roberts -- C. H. Repath -- C. V. Hopkins--Tom Taylor and Robt E. Tally, all members of the United Verde Copper Company.

So, in 1910 Clark started buying up property at the bottom of Mingus Mountain where he would build his new smelter. In total, he purchased 1,200 acres in the Verde Valley including pristine land along the Verde River.

Verde River

Preceding the Town of Clarkdale, this region had natural grasses, orchards, farm land and plenty of water. The economy was based predominantly on agriculture and ranching.

Clark needed a better way to get supplies in to build his new company town and the copper out to market. He financed a railroad along the Verde River where Mother Nature had already carved a path.

Construction of this 38-mile standard gauge line began in October 1911 and was completed in November 1912 at a cost of $3.5 million.

The Ore Train ran between
Hopewell and Clarkdale

The operation included the construction of a new smelter at Clarkdale, a new surface plant on the 500' level elevation of the mine, the installation of new underground hoisting facilities and shafts, the development of a tunnel transfer system known as the "Hopewell Tunnel" on the one thousand foot level and the construction of the Verde Tunnel and Smelter Railroad.

This standard gauge line initially ran from the portal of the Hopewell tunnel, where ore from the mine was transferred to 40-ton bottom-dump railroad cars for transport to the Clarkdale smelter.

The 38 miles of standard-gauge railway was built. This rail line connected to the Atchison, Topeka and Santa Fe Railway mainline to a branch near Drake which ran to the Clarkdale depot, then on to the Hopewell Tunnel.

Clarkdale Depot Circa 1915

Clarkdale Smelter

The Clarkdale smelter started operation in 1915. This smelter included six roasting furnaces, three 19 by 101 foot reverberatory furnaces, four 48 by 320 inch blast furnaces and four 12 foot diameter converters. The United Verde Company erected a 400 foot steel smoke stack.

At that time it was reported to be the world's tallest steel stack.

The copper-laden ore was crushed and ground to a fine size, prior to concentrating it by a froth flotation process. The concentrate was then roasted to drive off excess sulfur before being fed to the smelter to recover the copper.

The toxic smoke and fumes from the nearby smelter coughed up 935 tons of sulfur dioxide and 100 tons of metal-laden smoke per day poisoning and killing off most of the vegetation in the surrounding area.

Clarkdale residents said the smoke from the smelter constantly burned their eyes. They smelled it, tasted it and even felt it.

The molten slag, a stony waste matter formed from impurities was separated from metals during the refining of the ore and was dumped in a pile. Once cooled, it becomes extremely hard and shiny. The Clarkdale slag pile occupies an area of approximately 45 acres, with a consistent thickness of around 100 feet. The slag pile is located between the Verde River and the railroad tracks.

In addition, the leftover froth or tailings slurry consisting of fine sand, pyrite and toxic heavy metals was pumped through miles of redwood pipes to a couple of large tailing ponds located near Tuzigoot National Monument, the once pre-historic farmland of the Sinagau Indians. It is estimated that the toxic slurry ponds were 50 feet deep in places.

The once pristine, green valley soon looked like a wasteland. The smelting operation resulted in deforestation of most of the large vegetation and severely impacted the local farmers' crops.

After the mining operation closed, the ponds dried out and the orange toxic copper dust would blow in the wind. To help this problem, they ran sprinklers to keep it wet. Finally, in 2006 the tailings were covered with soil and planted over with native vegetation. The Rain Spirit RV Resort now occupies part of that site.

This is a newspaper article regarding the dust from the tailing ponds.

Verde Independent; May 5, 1955

"Orange dust is blowing hundreds of feet into the sky and streaming out for miles on windy days. The almost daily dust storm is not too choosy when it comes to direction. Clarkdale, Cottonwood, and even Cornville have lain in its path on different days during the past month. Housewives as well as storekeepers are keeping late hours cleaning up the dust. At Tuzigoot they are scraping the stuff off furniture by the handful and tourists are turning away from Tuzigoot in droves."

Clarkdale Main Street

Clark's United Verde Copper Company owned everything in town, the streets, the schools, the buildings and most of the businesses.

The town included a business block built in 1914 which is largely still intact on Main Street today. All places of business were housed in modern brick buildings. The Gassoway drug store on Main Street was very popular.

Noticeably, due to prohibition at the time, there were no bars or saloons in town.

Gassoway Drug Store

Children would rush to the candy counter filled with jelly beans and candy corn. The adult's would sit at the soda bar drinking a Coca-Cola, while in the back room the pharmacist would be grinding medicinal herbs and compounds to fill the orders for home remedies and prescriptions.

For those pesky intestinal worms, folks used St. Joseph's Worm Syrup. For the teething babies it was Mrs. Winslow Soothing Syrup. For coughs, a couple of bottles of Piso Cure would do the trick. For a stomach ache, some used Jamaica Ginger.

Clarkdale had a pool hall, three grocery stores, two dry-goods stores, two cafes, two cigar stores, a furniture store, a music store, a laundry, the Arizona Bank, a moving picture theater and a swimming pool that was marked **"WHITE ONLY."**

Clarkdale Home on Main Street

All homes were rented from the company and they strictly policed everything. Among others, there were rules like; no nails in the walls or chopping wood on the porch.

And if an employee's child became out of control, their parents could be subject to disciplinary actions.

Golf Course at Peck's Lake

In the 1920's the Verde Valley Country Club and a nine-hole golf course on Peck's Lake was built. **As you moved down the hill you moved down in status.** Clarkdale was a segregated town for much of its early history. Upper Clarkdale was designated for engineers, executives and white-collar officials. Lower Clarkdale was for the Anglo class workers. Mexican laborers were restricted to living in Patio Town and the Chinese population was located near the Verde River.

These laborers performed some of the hardest jobs, such as mining, railroad work and laundry services. There were many ethnic groups working for the company and they separated themselves for many reasons. First, their skill sets was different. Second, their language was different. Third their customs and food choices were different. And forth, not surprisingly, even their vice of choice was different.

The Chinese smoked opium and the Mexicans smoked marijuana.

The Germans drank beer and the Russians drank vodka. The Italians made wine and the Irish made whiskey.

Prohibition in Arizona went into effect on January 1, 1915, just as the Town of Clarkdale was being built. But this law did not stop the appetite for these vices. They just went underground. Speakeasies, moonshiners, and, Bootleggers began to pop up everywhere.

The term, bootlegger came from folks who hid liquor in their boots in order to smuggle it to customers. The term Moonshiner comes from folks that made the illegal liquor often by the light of the moon.

Arizona Territory

Chapter Three

Let us go back even further and explore the Wild West when Arizona was still a territory. This will give us a little context on how the town of Clarkdale came about.

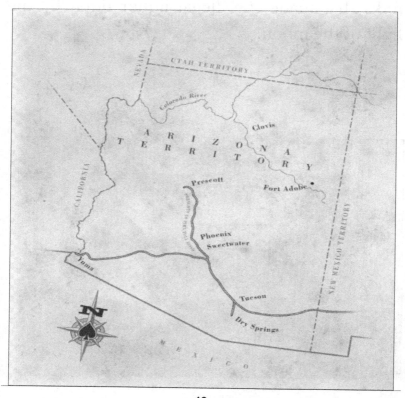

Arizona became a part of the federal union in 1850 when New Mexico Territory became part of the United States. The treaty of Guadalupe Hidalgo ended the Mexican-American war.

Our neighboring town, Prescott was founded one year later in 1864 as the Territorial Capital.

At that time, the population of Arizona was about 80% men and 20% women.

Virgil Earp lived in Prescott and was appointed as the Deputy Marshal of the Arizona Territory in 1879.

By 1880 the discovery of gold near Prescott had the Arizona territory crawling with fortune seekers.

In November of that year, the famous outlaw **Billy the Kid** was up in Jerome drinking whiskey in Nora Brown's Saloon. Billy was trying to keep the patrons distracted. Unbeknownst to the patrons, Billy had hired a local band of Yavapai Apache Indians that were camped along the river in what is now called Clarkdale.

The Indians were paid to steal the patron's horses from Jerome's livery stable.

Billy almost got into a gun fight with Virgil's younger brother, the more famous **Wyatt Earp** who was also a patron at Nora Brown's saloon that night. Billy managed to pull off the raid and got away with several horses.

This event is well documented by both William Wingfield, a long-time rancher in the Verde Valley who happened to be in the saloon that night along with Nora Brown herself.

True West Magazine has an article on this story.

Back in those days the only thing dry in Arizona was its deserts. Beer and whiskey were very popular and some thought even safer than the water.

It's true that most of the water in these arid towns was of poor quality and without refrigeration; people drank either warm beer or straight liquor like rye or bourbon. Whiskey was sold by the shot and beer by the mug.

Often, dad would send his child, to a local saloon with an empty bucket in hand, to fetch a "growler" of beer. As the child traveled back home, the beer inside the bucket would jostle. The carbonated gases would expand and push their way out of the lid making a growling noise, thus giving the bucket of beer the name growler.

It's not surprising that one of the very first and most profitable enterprises in any Arizona town was a saloon. Most of their whiskey and beer was made on location and kept cool in an underground cellar or storage room.

The towns grew and soon a local government was created. Next thing you knew, saloon owners had to purchase a license to operate. Hungry for more money, the newly formed government placed a sales tax on every drink sold. Sound familiar?

This revenue often paid for a local sheriff and became a major source of income for most small towns.

As more and more people moved into these Wild West towns, the drinking population wanted more whiskey.

The distillers back East began shipping whiskey to all sorts of colorful towns including Laramie, Dodge City, Tombstone and Jerome.

Most of the liquors were transported in wooden barrels. A 16-gallon keg weighed 140 pounds, as much as most men and was hard to handle.

Once the wooden barrels arrived at a saloon, a dishonest saloon owner would water down the whiskey by adding color, moonshine, tobacco and other dubious ingredients all to extend his profits. Then he would transfer the liquor into existing containers.

The horrible stories about people going blind after drinking bootleg liquor are true. Tainted booze may have killed more than 10,000 people before the repeal of the 18th Amendment.

Until the "Bottled-in-Bond" act of 1897, you might find all kinds of crap in your drink. This meant that the distillery was under government supervision and the whiskey was certified to be free of other additives.

A good number of the saloons were like social clubs where a man could hear the latest news, buy or sell livestock, hire a strong-armed boy to do a little dirty work or bribe a few voters with shots of whiskey. These saloons served customers like cowboys, outlaws, prospectors and even politicians.

Women for the most part were not permitted in saloons unless they were dancing girls or serving drinks. Truth is, most of these girls doubled as prostitutes and were looked down upon by society.

On the other side, religious revivalists and early teetotaler groups like the Anti-Saloon League and the Women's Christian Temperance Union campaigned against what they viewed as a nationwide plague of drunkenness. Calls for a "dry" America continued on Capitol Hill until prohibition.

Prohibition wouldn't be complete without a tribute to Kansas's most colorful woman, the famed Carry Nation.

Carry Nation's first husband, who was a severe alcoholic, drank himself to death. She then married David Nation, who soon divorced her because of her insane ways of showing her hatred for liquor.

Carry would walk into a saloon, fly into a rage and with a hatchet, destroy everything in sight. She had a large following of women that also despised liquor. Ultimately, Carry was arrested 35 times for her attacks on saloons. The hatchet became her trade mark.

Arizona had its own out-spoken loyalists, a woman named **Frances Lillian Willard.** Frances Willard was a great admirer of Carry Nation. Willard Avenue in Cottonwood is named after her family. Miss Willard moved from California to  the Arizona territory and worked as a school teacher. She taught school in the Mormon town of Pine and traveled around to teach in several other small towns such as Cottonwood, Clarkdale, Payson and Jerome. Her lesson plans included promoting the evils of alcohol to her young students.

Frances Lillian Willard married John Lee Munds. (John Munds was a sheriff for Cottonwood Jerome and Clarkdale.) Frances worked tirelessly for women's suffrage.

The women's right to vote in Arizona was granted in November 1912, almost a decade before the passage of the 19th Amendment nationwide. She was the first woman elected to the Arizona Senate and the second woman elected to the United States Senate. She served Arizona as Senator from 1915 to 1917.

With her leadership and the women's vote, on January 1, 1915 prohibition went into effect and the whole state of Arizona went dry.

Without Frances (Willard) Munds influencing the women's vote, Arizona would not have become a dry state until five years later when the 18th Amendment, (Prohibition) went into effect nationwide.

Clarkdale's business block was being built that very same year. With prohibition now in effect statewide, and to the disappointment of a lot of people, there would be no saloons or bars built in the town of Clarkdale.

However, the amendment did not outlaw the drinking of alcohol. It only prohibited the manufacture, sale or transportation of liquor, not its consumption.

Oh Please Say It Isn't So

Chapter Four

From 1915 to 1933, the local newspapers during prohibition were full of reported arrests by brave Yavapai County sheriffs during the prohibition era. John Munds, Fred Hawkins, Ed Weil and Jim Roberts were among the most influential.

Sheriff
Jonnie Munds

He had more
than a fews
opportunities
To find himsrlf
in coflict with the
Moonshiners
and Bootleggers

John Munds was elected Sheriff of Yavapai County on the Democratic ticket for two terms. Johnnie, as they called him was the husband of aforementioned Frances Willard. She was a "teetotaler" and helped Arizona become a dry state.

There is no doubt that his wife, Frances and her abhorrence for liquor had an influence on how Johnnie Munds enforced the 18th amendment. He was the son of a Cottonwood rancher named William Munds. Munds Park near Flagstaff is named after this early ranching family.

Fred
Hawkins

He would disarm
a man if he could,

Wound him if
that's what it took
to subdue him

And only kill if he
must.

Fred Hawkins was a tall slender man. He had a sandy moustache that drooped a bit on each side of his mouth. He had a long career, first as Deputy Marshal of Jerome, then deputy sheriff of the Clarkdale precinct during the prohibition era. He had more than a few opportunities to find himself in conflict with the moonshiners and bootleggers.

People that knew him said, Fred Hawkins would disarm a man if he could, wound him if that's what it took to subdue him and only kill if he must.

Sheriff
Ed Weil
He was called
"The two-gun
sheriff

Ed Weil was another interesting Sheriff of Yavapai County during the height of prohibition. He was called "The Two-Gun Sheriff". He wore a pair of Colt six-shooters, one on each hip and he didn't monkey around.

Some said, the seized copper still collection in his office almost rivaled the entire production of the big copper mines in Jerome.

Anywhere there was moonshine still; he just simply went and confiscated it. It didn't matter if it was up on the mountain in Jerome, down by the river in Clarkdale, or out on a deserted ranch in the valley.

Sheriff Weil said, "I've got a big Studebaker automobile loaded to the brim with copper stills and a dozen more places to raid. I need room to store the copper somewhere else. I'm running a sheriff's office, not a copper storage warehouse."

Sheriff
Jim Roberts

He served as a
Lawman for 40 years.
He is famous for the
capture of two
Oklahoma bank robbers
who held up the
Bank of Arizona in
Clarkdale Arizona
and seized the
United Verde Copper Co
payroll of $ 64,000.

Jim Roberts worked as an Arizona lawman for 40 years between 1893 and 1934. Jim Roberts was the "last sheriff standing" in the Pleasant Valley War and one of Arizona's greatest lawman.

Roberts didn't swear, drink, play cards or dress like a cowboy. He rode a mule instead of a horse and he didn't look or act the part of a legendary gun fighter. Roberts carried his nickel-plated six shooter in his hip pocket instead of a tanned leather holster. His gun looked like it had not been fired in decades.

Some even questioned his authenticity, but all those doubts came to rest in the summer of 1928. Deputy Jim Roberts was walking a foot-beat in downtown Clarkdale.

Two criminals out of Oklahoma parked their stolen vehicle in front of the Bank of Arizona on Main Street and entered the Clarkdale bank with firearms. The bandits forced all the bank employees into the vault and collected a gunny sack containing over $40,000 in United Verde Mine payroll. It was the largest heist in Arizona's history at that time.

The bandits jumped into their getaway car. Deputy Roberts saw the two bandits speed away just as he rounded the corner. One of the bandits fired his gun out of the car window at lawman Roberts. Roberts reached into his hip pocket, took out his six shooter and carefully took aim. He held the gun steady with his aging, wrinkled hands. He fired twice, striking the driver in the back of the head.

The car skidded sideways striking a telephone pole guy wire. The vehicle crashed and Roberts captured the other bandit. The money was recovered. That was **Jim Robert**'s last gun fight.

The Lawman died a few years later while walking a beat on the Clarkdale Street.

Here is a letter sent to the authorities from the wife of a regular moonshine customer. The address is Third Street, Lower Town. The date stamped on it is September 20 1931. It reads.

"Dear Sir, My husband is in the habit of buying a quart of whiskey every other day from a Chinese bootlegger named Chin. I believe the Chinaman lives near the Verde River. We need this money for household expenses. Will you please have his place raided? He keeps a supply planted in the garden and a smaller quantity under the back steps for quick delivery. If you make the raid before 9:30 in the morning you'll be sure to get the goods. Thank you in advance, Yours Truly, Mrs. Jack Hillyer"

Prescott Arizona's First News Paper Office
The Prescott Weekly Miner

The early local newspapers from 1915 to 1930 were full of reported arrests by the brave Yavapai Sheriffs. Clarkdale alone had hundreds of arrests and violations. Here are just nine examples.

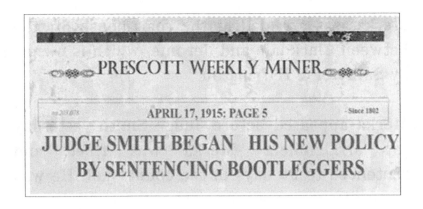

PRESCOTT WEEKLY MINER

APRIL 17, 1915: PAGE 5   - Since 1802

JUDGE SMITH BEGAN   HIS NEW POLICY BY SENTENCING BOOTLEGGERS

Prescott Weekly Miner April 1915

The Prescott Weekly Miner Newspaper reported that **Clarkdale was actually the first town in Yavapai County** caught violating the prohibition law just a few weeks after the law went into effect in April of 1915.

Judge Smith immediately implemented his new policy by sentencing bootleggers to fines and even hard time.

Frank Merka, who despite the 'dry' law thought he would assist in keeping Arizona 'wet. Merka had a side business in moonshining and bootlegging that gets him in trouble with the law.

Merka was arrested at the road house Station between Clarkdale and Jerome, which is owned by Sullivan & Harrington.

Merka appeared before Judge Smith yesterday for arraignment. Merka was fined and sentenced to 90 days in the county jail. He was fined $100 to be worked out with hard labor on the basis of $1 per day. Judge Smith announced it will be the rule of the court for any convicted persons. This will act as a warning to all offenders and at the same time assist the county materially, as men are needed to put the county roads into proper shape for the summer.

PRESCOTT WEEKLY MINER

DECEMBER 7, 1917 — Since 1802

BOOZE CACHE DISCOVERED IN CLARKDALE

Prescott Weekly Miner December 1917

The Deputy Sheriff made quite a haul of bootleg whiskey in Clarkdale on Friday afternoon; about 225 pints of high-grade whiskey was seized when the home of Mike Lamarich, an Austrian smelter worker, was raided by the officer and his assistants.

Mike Lamarich, having been tipped off regarding the raid, made haste to get out of town and has not been seen since that day.

One of the peculiar circumstances of the raid was the somewhat unusual manner in which the man had his illicit possessions cached away in various parts of his house.

Some of the bottles were found buried in the family sugar supply and others were dug out of the flour barrel.

The bulk of the booze, however, was found in a secret room beyond the cellar wall. More than 200 bottles of liquor were found in this receptacle. Besides the whiskey, two barrels of wine were captured by the raiders.

Officer Bartlett brought the cargo to this city yesterday afternoon, and it is now reposing in one of the cells in the county jail.

THE COCONINO SUN

no.203.074 | JANUARY 10,1919: PAGE 7 | - Since 1802

SHERIFF JOHN MUNDS SHOOTS A SIX SHOOTER OUT OF THE HANDS OF A BOOTLEGGER

The Coconino Sun 1919

Deputy Sheriff Johnnie Munds engaged with an alleged bootlegger near Clarkdale. Munds had learned that a shipment of liquor was to come into the district. It wasn't long until he noticed an unknown stranger driving a car.

Munds stopped the driver and ordered him to get out of the car. The driver later known as Clements, instead of obeying, ducked behind his companion and drew his gun on the sheriff.

Sheriff Munds, being quick on the trigger, did a remarkable piece of shooting. He shot the pistol out of Clements's grasp, inflicting a painful though not serious wound in the man's right hand. That shot ended all attempts at resistance on the part of the bootleggers. Both men were brought to the Jerome jail.

Officers took a deeper look at the car and after some prodding and poking found two slits in the upholstery in the back seat.

Below the slits were two galvanized tanks with holes cut in the tops large enough to permit a man to reach in and extract a quart of whiskey for a passing customer. 113 bottles of amber fluid were found tucked away beneath the seats.

PRESCOTT EVENING COURIER

MAY 4, 1921: PAGE 1   Since 1802

SHERIFF FRED HAWKINS FOUND THE NINTEENTH HOLE ON VERDE GOLF COURSR IN CLARKDALE

Prescott Evening Courier 1921

Deputy Sheriff Fred Hawkins and Constable Ray Byers are said to have located the 19th hole on the Verde Golf Course near the upper end of Pecks Lake. Dug into the bank of the Verde River was a 1000' foot tunnel.

All Saturday afternoon Hawkins and Byers waded along an icy four-foot stream with electric flashlights. About, half way in from the portal, there was some slight evidence that the tunnel had been disturbed.

The officers tore away the plaster and an underground distillery lay open in a chamber above the roof. The chamber held a large moonshine operation including a large kerosene stove. Discovered were several gallon jugs of whiskey, six barrels filled with mash and about 1000 pounds of corn, not yet ground.

All the equipment was taken to Clarkdale on the first stage of its journey to Prescott. The corn will be distributed among the poor families of Clarkdale.

PRESCOTT EVENING COURIER

JANUARY 28, 1924 : PAGE 2   Since 1802

"TONY CANOVAS, OF CLARKDALE,
PLEADED GUILTY WHEN CALLED
BEFOR PHOENIX FEDERAL COURT"

Prescott Evening Courier 1924

For all intents and purposes, Tony Canovas was running a normal Italian restaurant. His food however, was used as a lure to coax his customers into buying his bootlegged wine in which he specialized.

Canovas, who was known as the "King of the Verde Valley Bootleggers" was caught by federal agents as the result of a dragnet raid extending from one end of the valley to the other.

At his "hog ranch" which was about half way between Clarkdale and Jerome and handy to both towns, the most complete moonshine operation in this county was discovered.

In raiding the place, the agents discovered a storage room made entirely of concrete located underneath the hog pens. The entrance to this underground room was down a well and through a tunnel.

Agents found several barrels of wine and a complete wine making operation. Canovas pleaded guilty to four charges, one for manufacturing and three for possession. He was fined $404 and sentenced to serve four months in the Maricopa County Jail.

PRESCOTT EVENING COURIER

AUGUST 5, 1929

"COPS NAB A BIG WHISKEY CARGO NEAR JEROME, BUT JUST COULDN'T KEEP CURLEY IN HOOSEGOW"

Prescott Evening Courier 1929

R. E. Reese, better known as "Curly" according to the cops was a professional bootlegger and had been receiving car loads of moonshine from Gallup, New Mexico and reselling it.

He was captured early in the morning of April 26, 1929 with 5 cases of booze in his car and had ten cases of booze hidden in the rocks near Clarkdale.

Deputy Marshal Fred Hawkins and Policeman Charles Smith placed Reese in the Clarkdale Jail.

Mrs. Reese visited him at the jail about 5 o'clock in the afternoon and asked Officer Twitty to hold him there until morning, stating that she would be able to raise his bail bond.

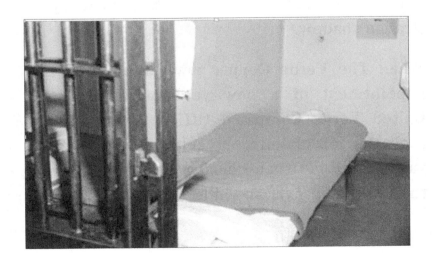

The next morning, when Officer Twitty went to feed the prisoners, he found Reese's cell empty.

Someone had made entrance into the jail house that night by sawing through the back door. The padlock on Reese's cell was also sawed through and the way to the library lay open.

"The Jailbird, known as Curly has flown the coop," announced Officer Fred Twitty. It is believed that Curly may be hiding somewhere in the hills between Clarkdale and Jerome.

After this jail break, Officer Fred Twitty always felt that he was being stalked by a strange shadow.

When The Verde Copper news announced the appointment of a new yard master for the United Verde Company, Officer Twitty gladly took the job claiming he felt safer taking the yardmaster job than chasing bootleggers down the valley and over the hills.

Ghost Town Tours LLC of Jerome provides historic shuttle tours as well as a fully interactive ghost adventure in the Verde Valley. One of their agents interviewed a former Clarkdale Police Officer who worked for the department.

The officer said he had unexplainable experiences over the years while working at the jail. He claimed he had seen apparitions, smelled a strange stench of liquor from an unknown source and often heard the sound of someone sawing through metal.

Could it have been the ghost of a bootlegger trying to escape jail? Or maybe it was former Officer Fred Twitty's ghost still coming in to do his shift.

Because officers are trained to focus on the naturally occurring dangers of the job, it is hard for many them to accept the existence of ghosts. You can probably see why this former officer was a little reluctant to share his story.

But, if you think bootlegging, moon shining or trafficking in opium was the sole domain of men, you have only to examine the records of the Yavapai County Sheriff's Office to be convinced otherwise. Clarkdale had another first. For the first time in the history of the Superior Court of Yavapai County, a woman is charged with violation of the prohibition amendment, an offense more popularly known as "bootlegging".

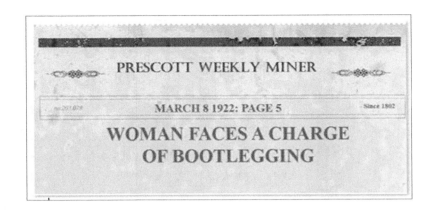

PRESCOTT WEEKLY MINER

MARCH 8 1922: PAGE 5   Since 1862

WOMAN FACES A CHARGE OF BOOTLEGGING

<u>Prescott Weekly Miner 1922</u>

Mary Orlich, of Clarkdale, admitted the sale of a quart bottle of brandy to Fisher J. Morris for the sum of $2.50. It's rumored that selling liquor was a common practice of hers.

Mary Orlich, who acted as her own attorney, entered a plea of guilty. She was sentenced to ten days in jail and fined $250.

The court named Deputy Sheriff Joe Cook of Clarkdale as her probation officer.

PRESCOTT EVENING COURIER

JANUARY 7, 1924: PAGE 1   ~Since 1802

WASH WOMAN PLEADS GUILTY OF MOONSHINNING

Prescott Evening Courier, 1924

Here's one about "money laundering." January 1924, Prescott Evening Courier: Wash Woman Pleads Guilty of moonshining.

Mrs. Felipe Medina, a wash woman living in Patio Town, was carrying one small child and leading another by the hand when she walked into the court room. Mrs. Medina pleaded guilty to a charge of selling moonshine.

Apparently, she had been charging a little extra for her laundry service by hiding bottles of bootlegged whiskey in the clean folded laundry.

When the court asked her if she owned any property, she said, "Only a whole lot of children." It was evident she was very poor.

Judge Jacobs's advice to her was to cut out the "money laundering" and bootlegging and devote her energies instead to laundering clothes.

The Judge fined her one dollar.

Verde Copper News 1918

A miscellaneous collection of bootleggers, slackers, thieves and murderers sat on the prisoners benches awaiting sentencing.

Among the prisoners was Miss Lucille Ellwood of Clarkdale. Miss Ellwood had entered a plea of guilty to a charge of having opium in her possession.

Judge Sawtelle called Miss Ellwood, who was a pretty girl of 21 years of age and dressed in stylish attire to step forward. He then asked her to explain how she had gotten into the clutches of opium smoking.

Lucille alleged that most of the opium that the Chinese used came from other Chinamen and that it would be pretty hard to say just how it was brought into the state.

She told the court that she had married a Chinaman named, Al Fee several months ago in New Mexico. She said, Al Fee owned a laundry in Clarkdale and lived near the Verde River. Judge Sawtelle asked the girl whether it was against the New Mexico law for a Celestial and a Caucasian to unite in marriage.

She replied. Mr. Al Fee and I are man and wife.

Judge Sawtelle paroled the young girl, with the understanding that she return to her parent's home on the west coast

.

Lucille said, "I'll go back to California, but I will return".

She said, "The longer you try to keep us apart, the stronger my love will be for the man of my choice. I actually don't care a snap of this little finger what anybody says or thinks".

Well, four months later the headline read
"Murder Case in Lover's Triangle."

The Chinaman Ah Fee was shot and killed in the back room of his Clarkdale laundry by another Chinaman named Chin. Two sides of the lover's triangle were these two Chinese men. The third side of the triangle was Lucille Ellwood of Clarkdale. Apparently both Chinamen were in love with the young, attractive, American girl known as Lucy.

Old Timer's Gold Nuggets

Chapter Five

Not everyone worked for the copper mining company. There were other forms of making a living like farming, ranching and even prospecting. Here's a story about an old, 1920's prospector and his gold nuggets. An old prospector and his wife lived on a homestead in Sycamore Canyon, in Clarkdale near the Gold Tooth Mine. The prospector mostly kept to himself.

Every other week he would take his pack animals and head in to town for supplies. In the morning he would meet up with a few friends. In the afternoon, he would go to the assay office, reach deep into his pocket and bring out a small bag of gold dust and maybe a gold nugget or two and cash them in. He would then stop by the livery stable and buy a couple sacks of feed grain for his mule and some cracked corn for his chickens.

Next, he would go by the market and buy a few canning jars and some sugar for his wife before heading back into the canyon.

The word spread quickly about the old prospector's good fortune.

A couple cowboys had the idea to follow the old prospector, find his goldmine and stake their own claim nearby. Staying out of site, the cowboys followed the old prospector to his mine down in Sycamore Canyon. They watched as the prospector took his supplies from the pack saddle and carried them into a cave located along the banks of Sycamore Creek. They stayed out of sight until the prospector went back to his shack.

When the coast was clear and by the light of the moon, the cowboys entered the cave. To their surprise, it wasn't a gold mine at all. Inside, the cave was an elaborate moonshine system.

The old prospector was making moonshine whiskey and selling it to the company miners in Jerome. The miners knew if they had tried to cash in the gold they had been high-grading from the copper mines, they would be fired for sure. Remember, this was during prohibition and the miners were mighty thirsty.

I guess you could say the old prospector did have a gold mine of sorts. Bootlegging moonshine was illegal, but profitable. Who knows if the prospector's story is true or not, but usually with every tale, there's a grain of truth.

Moonshiners were often sought after by law enforcement. More times than not, authorities had to track the alleged criminals on foot. Depending on the location, sometimes a fresh set of human foot prints would be suspicious and indicative of people brewing moonshine.

To avoid capture, some moonshiners strapped a carved piece of wood to the bottom of their shoes that left foot prints resembling cow tracks. This practice kept the revenuers guessing.

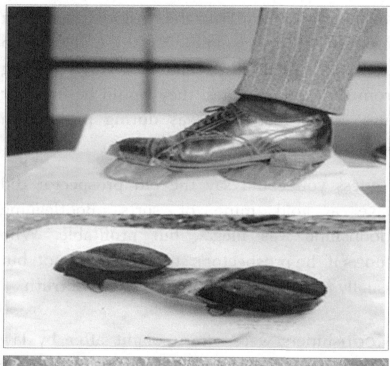

Henry's Horse Feed Hooch

Chapter six

It is said that when the immigrants came to this country, the English built churches, the Germans built barns and the Irish made whiskey in the back of barns.

My great, great grandfather, Joe Henry Jewell (Irish) and his wife Martha (Cherokee) and their five children lived on a small farm in Southern Tennessee.

From the stories I've heard; when asking directions to his home, Joe Henry would say, "Go down the county road until the road peters out."

When asked if he made money selling his hogs, Joe Henry would say, "Not so much, cuz we live where the road peters out."

When asked if he made money selling his horse feed moonshine, Joe Henry would say, "Not so much cuz we live were the road peters out."

Apparently, by the time a customer would get to his house, they had already spent all their money with other sellers or moonshiners along the way. After all, he lived way at the end, "where the road peters out"

 I have my great, great grandfather, Joe Henry's original, recipe for moonshine. One of my Great Aunts wrote it down just as he told it to her. He called it Henry's Horse Feed Hooch.

The recipe calls for sweet horse feed, home canned peaches and yeast.

The moonshine was delicious. It may be similar to the one the old prospector used.

The liquor will be between 150 and 180 proof. It has a slight nutty flavor with a hint of peach. This recipe should have yielded about two gallons of hooch. This hooch can be diluted with clean water.

The retail price for a quart of peach moonshine is about $ 25.00. It cost about $ 5.00 to make it. But a word of caution, making moonshine can be dangerous. Many homes and barns have been burnt to the ground. Alcohol is very combustible! It is also illegal without a permit. Today if you're caught selling hooch you could face a $10,000 fine and five years in the hoosegow.

I'll share it, but keep in mind this recipe is meant for entertainment purposes and anyone who actually follows through with it should be both admired for their ambition and mocked for their foolishness.

Henry's Horse Feed Hooch
Joe Henry Jewell-1922

<u>*Step 1:*</u>   **Build** *yur fire out back of the barn. Use hard wood chips to keep the smoke down so the revenuers won't find ya.*

Boil **4 gallons of rain water** *in a big copper kettle.*

Add a 5 lb sack of sugar *Stir with a clean hay fork or shovel till dissolved.*

Add 8 scoops of sweet horse feed. *Use the horse feed with several different grains like barley, oats, corn, wheat and molasses.*

Add a cake of yeast, *Dissolve in 2 gallons of warm rain water, not hot or yu'll kill the yeast.*

Add 2 quarts of canned peaches. *Keep the jar to fill with moonshine later.*

Mix it all together, *cover with a wet burlap feed sack to keep the flies and vermin out. Let it ferment a spell, sturin once in a while. It should be ready to run in about 5 days.* **At this stage,** *it's now sour mash. The mash is ready when it stops bubbling.*

Strain through a pillow cover, but not the ones with the fancy stichen cuz Ma will be mad and ya. You want to stay on her good side if ya want to eat her fine cookin'. Keep the liquid and feed the grain to yur hogs. Sometimes the hogs get a little drunk, but they love the Hooch soaked grain.

Step 2: Now, yur ready to run the liquid in yur copper still. Put this newly fermented sour mash liquid into the cooker and carefully bring it up to exactly *170 degrees Fahrenheit.*

All connections need to be tight when under heat. Seal any leaks with a rye flour paste. **Run most** of the copper coils through cold water.

As the vapors pass through the cold copper tubing, they condense into a clear liquid.

Step 3: Place the opposite end into a funnel with another fine filter and dispense it into a jug or mason jar.

Keep repeating the process and yu'll have a steady supply of hooch fur yourself and a few of yur rite close friends.

If ya messed up, ya go blind or die a slow death and if yur caught by the revenuers, ya go to jail.

Some folks call it White Lightning or Mountain Dew or Moonshine or Rotgut, but I call it **Hooch.**

Joe Henry

The Volstead Act

Chapter Seven

The Volstead Act was passed in 1921. Prohibition however, did include a few interesting exceptions. Sacramental wine was permitted for religious purposes and drug stores were allowed to sell "medicinal whiskey" to treat everything from toothaches to the flu. Drugstores and pharmacy chains suddenly become a very lucrative business.

With alcohol becoming illegal nationwide, it prompted consumers to search for substitutes. With a doctor's order, patients could legally buy a pint of hard liquor every few days. The pharmaceutical booze often came with seemingly laughable doctor's order such as;

"Take three ounces every hour for stimulant until stimulated."

It was the golden age of secret remedies, quacks, false cures and snake oils. One could pick up almost any of these remedies at the local drug store on Main Street in Clarkdale or get your doctor to give you a prescription for "Medicinal Whiskey".

This practice is verified by some of the bottles dug up right here in the various Clarkdale dumps. Above is a photo of one of the bottles.

Here is a little history on this product. Patented medicines with a high alcohol percentage, such as Jamaica Ginger, often called "Jake" were 90 proof.

It became an obvious choice, as it was legal and available over the counter for about 35 cents without a prescription.

In 1920, the U.S. Treasury Department required manufactures to modify the Jamaica Ginger recipes with a higher concentration of ginger solids, resulting in an incredibly bitter taste and made it almost impossible to drink.

The Jamaica Ginger Company decided to add a chemical plasticizer to increase the solids in the bottle.

This chemical was odorless and tasteless. It did the trick by adding more solids into the bottle. But, something was amiss. Blues and folk songs of the day picked up on this, describing drinkers of the Jamaica Ginger as having something the people coined as **"Jake Leg" or "Jake Walk."**

Large numbers of Jamaica Ginger drinkers began to lose muscle control. Their toes flopped as they walked making a slapping sound on the ground. This very peculiar gait became known as the **Jake Walk**.

It was later discovered that the ingredient the company added contained a neurotoxin. People were slowly being poisoned as the brew attacked the cells in the spinal column. It is estimated that some **50,000** people were crippled as a result of drinking Jamaica Ginger, aka "Jake"

.

Ginger Paralysis:
Syndrome & Cause

- Characterized by ataxia, muscular weakness, unsteady gait, flaccid paralysis of the legs.
- Also known as jake leg, wrist drop, and foot drop.
- Caused by exposure to TOCP, with delayed onset of 1 to 3 weeks.

Several green bottles of Piso Cure have also been found. This medicine was sold at the Clarkdale Drug Store as a cure for everything from sore throats to sore toes and even Tuberculosis, also known as "Consumption".

This is the very product that the ladies were buying for their cough, caused by the smelter smoke. The majority of the customers for this medicine were women. It soon became one of America's best-selling patented medicines. The company advertised this product on a national level.

In 1920, Norman Rockwell, the famous American illustrator was commissioned to make an advertising poster to help the sale of this product. One poster reads; "Good for Young and Old". Once you recognize the ingredients, you'll understand why the people felt better after taking Piso Cure.

At various times, Piso's Cure contained opium, morphine, hashish, marijuana, chloroform and alcohol.

As soon as its affects wore off, you would need another dose. The user soon became addicted. If you find one of these little green bottles in an old dump the chances of finding more in the same spot is a given.

Here is another bottle that contains a disturbing remedy. It was also dug up from a Clarkdale dump. It was called Mrs. Winslow's Syrup for cutting teeth.

The ad reads: "ADVICE TO MOTHERS

"Are you broken in your rest by a sick child suffering with the pain of cutting teeth? Go at once to a chemist and get a bottle of Mrs. Winslow's Soothing Syrup.

It is perfectly harmless and pleasant to taste. It soothes the child; it softens their gums and allays all pain. It is the best-known remedy for diarrhea. The little cherub will awake as bright as a button".

ADVICE TO MOTHERS.

MRS. WINSLOW'S SOOTHING SYRUP,

should always be used for children teething. It soothes the child, softens the gums, allays all pain, cures wind colic, and is the best remedy for diarrhœa.

Twenty-Five Cents a Bottle.

Mothers would rub a little bit of this sweet syrup on their baby's gums. Just a teaspoonful of the syrup would have contained enough morphine to kill the average child, so it isn't hard to understand why so many babies who were given Mrs. Winslow's Soothing Syrup went to sleep and never woke up again.

It's also not hard to understand why this syrup was given the nickname, **"The Baby Killer"**.

But it wasn't just Jamaica Ginger, Piso Cure or Mrs. Winslow's Syrup that contained narcotics.

Coca-Cola was originally marketed as a patented medicine for headaches and physical exhaustion.

The name Coca-Cola was derived from two primary ingredients: the Coca leaf and the Kola nut. Extract of the Coca leaf was essentially Cocaine, and the Kola nut provided caffeine.

In the 1890s, Coke was directly marketed as a medicinal drink.

A bottle of Coke contained about 9 milligrams of cocaine and by comparison, the average line of cocaine equals about 50 milligrams.

It's not surprising the recipe was a closely kept secret. While the dosages were small, they were certainly habit-forming and soda fountains stood to profit from such consistent customers.

During prohibition, people couldn't go to bars anymore, so they turned to soda bars, aka soda fountains. The Gassoway Drug Store on Main Street in Clarkdale had a soda bar.

Drinking a bottle of cocaine-laced Coke wouldn't necessarily have gotten you high, but you surely would have felt a little pep in your step. Coca-Cola didn't become completely cocaine-free until 1929. This was the same year the stock market crashed, which brought on the Great Depression.

Soda fountains were one thing, but what most America men really wanted was beer. In 1933 the 18th Amendment was repealed with the 21st Amendment.

At the end of prohibition, our thirty second president, Franklin D. Roosevelt who served three terms, said, "What America needs is a drink."

Soon after prohibition, Congress placed a tax on alcohol; this tax is sometimes called the Sin Tax.

In the years between 1934 and 1964, liquor bottles had to be embossed with the phrase.

**"FEDERAL LAW FORBIDS
SALE OR RE-USE
OF THIS BOTTLE"**

This was done in an effort to discourage the reuse of empty bottles for bottling and selling homemade (moonshine) liquor. There are a lot of these discarded bottles with this phrase embossed on them in the old Clarkdale dumps. Later they used a paper labeled/ tax stamp on the bottles.

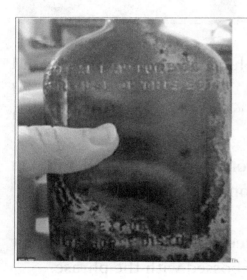

The "Federal Law Forbids Sale or Reuse of this Bottle"

Liquor, tobacco, lottery tickets and now marijuana have long been popular targets of taxation. Why? It's because, these products are highly taxed and our government collects millions of dollars on them. This tax is often called the "Sin Tax".

The reality is; it has nothing to do with morality or public safety. It's simply about how much money the government can extract from the use of these vises. The core reason that moonshine is illegal is because the government doesn't get their liquor tax, period.

Close the Town Down

Chapter Eight

William Andrew Clark Sr. (January 8, 1839 – March 2, 1925) was an American politician and entrepreneur involved with mining, banking and railroads. Clark died at the age of 86 in his New York City mansion.

After William Clark's death in 1925, Clark's sons and grandsons oversaw the construction of a recreational facility for the town of Clarkdale known as the Clarkdale Memorial Club House. It was built as a memorial and was completed in 1928.

One year later in 1929, the United Verde Mining Company had built 500 houses in Clarkdale and the little town was thriving. But that was about to change.

In the fall of that same year, on Tuesday Oct 28, 1929 the stock market crashed, the price of copper plummeted and times got hard. As a result, in 1935 the United Verde Copper Company sold the Clarkdale smelter to Phelps Dodge for 21 million dollars. Almost immediately, the new company began laying-off employees.

The people living in the company owned homes had no equity in their homes, and were merely renting. Now without jobs they had no reason to stay. They moved away leaving empty homes behind.

The smelter shut down operations in June of 1951. However, the concentrator remained in operation through February of 1953 for the purpose of processing the remaining stockpile of copper-zinc ore.

The towns of Jerome and Clarkdale both suffered. The Copper Mine closed for good in 1953.

The population of both towns continued to
decline and soon became ghost towns.

In 1957 Clarkdale was incorporated as an
independent municipality. The town sought to
bring in new economic enterprises to Clarkdale.

After the mines in Jerome closed, the town was
acquired by Erle P. Halliburton, whose estate
sold it to the Westfield Corporation in 1959 for
$1 million in cash.

Cement plant in Clarkdale Arizona

The Salt River Materials Group owns approximately 3,000 acres in the foothills of Mingus Mountain in Clarkdale. The plant produces Portland cement, fly ash, and gypsum. In 1959 The American Cement Company won the contract to supply "low-heat" cement for construction of the massive Glen Canyon Dam on the Colorado River. The cement plant was built in Clarkdale and the town slowly began to re-establish itself. Today the cement plant employs more than 200 people.

Matt and Eva Pecharich opened the 10/12 **LOUNGE** on Main Street in Clarkdale in the late fifties. It has stood the test of time and is one of the few businesses that has survived over the many years.

The Moscow Mule was their signature drink in the sixties. The recipe calls for vodka, ginger beer and lime poured over ice and served in a copper mug. It must be served in a copper mug or it's just not a real Moscow Mule.

Try one and you'll be surprised just how refreshing this mixed drink can be.

By the way, the 10/ 12 bar has live music on most weekends.

The Smelter Town Brewery and **Park Hotel** now occupies one of the historic buildings on Main Street and the **Clarkdale Kayak Company** has two river points for rafting on the Verde River

The Verde Canyon Railroad is an excursion train. It is hailed as North America's most scenic rail journey and not to be missed while visiting the area. The four hour journey takes visitors back in time as it winds along the banks of the Verde River. This train runs on a historic track between Clarkdale and the ghost town of Perkinsville on a 40-mile round trip.

Tuzigoot is a small, but interesting National Monument that reveals ruins of the 12th century Sinagua Indians, the first known people to inhabit the Verde Valley.

Clarkdale has two delightful museums.

The Clarkdale Historical Society Museum is located in the original medical clinic building. The police department was once located in the basement and that's where you will find the old jail. The museum has information about the "Model Town" of Clarkdale, including the Clark family history and the copper mining operation.

The Copper Art Museum is located in the Historic District of Clarkdale, Arizona and is in the old Clarkdale High School building. The museum has a dazzling array of gorgeous copper artifacts. A must see!

Today the little historic Town of Clarkdale, Arizona is making a comeback, but some of the town's historic buildings are still vacant.

Many of Clarkdale's original historic homes have been restored or rejuvenated.

Clarkdale's Town Park with its iconic gazebo and green grass serves as the focal point for events and concerts.

While visiting, take a drive through Clarkdale's quaint historic district and you'll notice the vintage boulevards and homes displaying a variety of architectural styles.

This outward charm once concealed an underlying social rigidity imposed on its residences. This social separation brought on by race, ethnicity and economic status would not be tolerated today.

Time has changed everything, especially people and what they value. Today, most residents of Clarkdale own their homes. Clarkdale has proved to be a destination for retirees and families. These residents tend to lean conservative and the public school in Clarkdale is above average.

Today the Town of Clarkdale is an all inclusive and welcoming community.

I'm not sure if there are any bootleggers still around, but Clarkdale does boast of some excellent restaurants, bars and wine tasting rooms for you to enjoy. It might be worth a try.

Historic Collection

Photos and Illustrations

- Libraries,
- Archives
- Personal Photos and Collections

News Papers

- Verde Heritage
- Prescott Weekly Miner
- Prescott Courier
- Coconino Sun
- Butte Miner
- Verde Copper News

References

Butte Montana Historical Society
P.O. Box 3913 Butte Mt. 59702

Clarkdale Historical Society and Museum
900 1st N. St. Clarkdale, Az. 86324

Sharlot Hall Museum
415 W. Gurley St. Prescott, Az. 86301

Jerome Historical Society
407 Clark Street Jerome, Az. 86331

Ghost Town Tours LLC of Jerome
403 Clark St A-2 Jerome, Az. 86331

Book References

They Came To Jerome, Billion Dollar Copper
Camp by Herbert V. Young

Clarkdale, Arizona. Engineering and Mining
Journal 104, No. 13   (September 29, 1917) by T.C.
Roberts,

Vision and Enterprise: Exploring the History of
Phelps Dodge Corporation. By Carlos A.
Schwantes

Empty Mansions: The Mysterious Life of
Huguette Clark by Bill Dedman and Paul Clark
Newell

Arizona Adventure, Action Packed True Tales of
Early Arizona by Marshall Trimble

About The Author

Peggy Hicks was born at home in rural Colorado. Being the oldest of ten siblings, she soon began telling imaginary tales to keep her little brothers and sisters amused.

At the early age of 12 years old, she published a short play that was purchased by the well-known educational publisher, Scott Foresman.

Growing up in the sixties, with guitar in hand, Peggy began turning her stories into poems and then into folk songs which she occasionally performed at local gatherings and auditoriums.

Peggy has since added many credits to her name as a musician, author, narrator and local historian. For several years she had the privilege of narrating the beautiful Verde Canyon Railroad scenic excursion.

Peggy has lived in Clarkdale for the past 30 years with her partner Dennis. Her love for storytelling based on legends and historical research has not diminished.

Books by Author

The Ghost of the Cuban Queen Bordello

Ghost Town Stories and Wicked Legends

Are Ghosts Real?

Bootleggers, Bottles and Badges

Contact Information
Peggy Hicks
callpeggy@swiftaz.net

Front Cover Photo

Moonshine on Bitter Creek

Made in United States
North Haven, CT
17 October 2023

42857838R00078